A Picture Book of Lewis and Clark

by David A. Adler   illustrated by Ronald Himler

Holiday House / New York

BRITISH TERRITORY

Fort Clatsop

WASHINGTON

Columbia River

CASCADE MOUNTAINS

Columbia River

OREGON

Snake River

Clearwater River

Salmon River

Lemhi River

Jefferson River

Madison River

MONTANA

Missouri River

Gallatin River

Yellowstone River

Fort Mandan

NORTH DAKOTA

MINNESOTA

Mississippi River

OREGON TERRITORY

IDAHO

WYOMING

SOUTH DAKOTA

Missouri River

North Platte

South Platte

ROCKY MOUNTAINS

NEBRASKA

Platte River

IOWA

Missouri River

St. Louis

St. Charles

SPANISH

TERRITORY

KANSAS

MISSOURI

Pacific Ocean

Mississippi River

New Orleans

Gulf of

On May 14, 1804, more than thirty American explorers began a journey into the unknown, into a land of mystery. They went west of the Mississippi River, where, some people said, woolly mammoths still roamed. They were the "Corps of Discovery" led by captains Meriwether Lewis and William Clark.

U N I T E D

S T A T E S

Mexico

Captain Meriwether Lewis was born on August 18, 1774, in Albermarle County, Virginia. His parents were William Lewis, a wealthy plantation owner, and Lucy Meriwether Lewis. He was the second of their three children.

In 1779, when Meriwether was just five, his father died. His mother married again, this time to Captain John Marks. In 1782 the family moved to the Georgia frontier. There Meriwether learned to live in the wilderness.

When he was thirteen, Meriwether returned to Virginia to help manage his family's plantation and go to school. At the age of twenty, he joined the Virginia militia and then the regular army.

Meriwether expected to remain a soldier, but in 1801 a Virginia neighbor wrote and asked him to be his secretary. "You would be one of my family."

The neighbor was Thomas Jefferson, the newly elected president of the United States.

Meriwether Lewis took the job.

As the president's secretary, he lived in the White House. In 1802 he and Jefferson began secret plans to explore the land beyond the western border of the United States. They hoped to find a water route across America, a Northwest Passage. Congress approved the mission and Jefferson appointed Lewis to lead it.

"The object of your mission," President Jefferson wrote to Lewis, "is to explore the Missouri River . . . and . . . the water offering the best communication with the Pacific Ocean." Jefferson also wanted to know about the land, weather, plants, and animals. He instructed Lewis to let the American Indians know "of our wish to be neighborly, friendly, and useful to them."

When the mission was planned, the land just west of the Mississippi River belonged to France. By the time it began, it belonged to the United States. On April 30, 1803, American agents sent to France by Jefferson bought the Louisiana Territory for the United States. The territory included all or parts of fifteen future states. It doubled the size of the United States.

Lewis traveled first to Philadelphia and then to Pittsburgh to prepare for the trip. He bought arms, ammunition, instruments, supplies, and gifts for the American Indians. He had a large keelboat built and also bought two smaller boats to carry all the supplies.

In June 1803 Captain Lewis wrote to Captain William Clark, an officer he had met during his service in the army. Lewis liked and respected Clark and asked him to help lead the expedition. "I do assure you," Clark wrote back, "that no man lives with whom I would prefer to undertake such a trip."

William Clark was born on August 1, 1770, in Caroline County, Virginia. His parents were John and Ann Rogers Clark. William was the ninth of their ten children, the youngest of six sons.

When William Clark was fourteen, his family moved to the American frontier, to Kentucky. There he learned to hunt, fish, camp, and find his way in the wilderness. When Clark was nineteen, he joined the army, where he learned to build forts, draw maps, and fight.

In mid October 1803 Lewis and Clark met on the north bank of the Ohio River in Clarksville, Indiana Territory, to prepare for their journey. They assembled men. Among them were Clark's slave, York, rivermen, and soldiers. They also took along Lewis's Newfoundland dog, Seaman. They spent the winter of 1803–1804 near St. Louis, Missouri, in a camp by the Mississippi River.

The Corps got under way on May 14, 1804, "under a gentle breeze," Clark wrote in his journal. They sailed across the Mississippi River and up the Missouri. Their journey across the American continent and back would take two years, four months, and ten days.

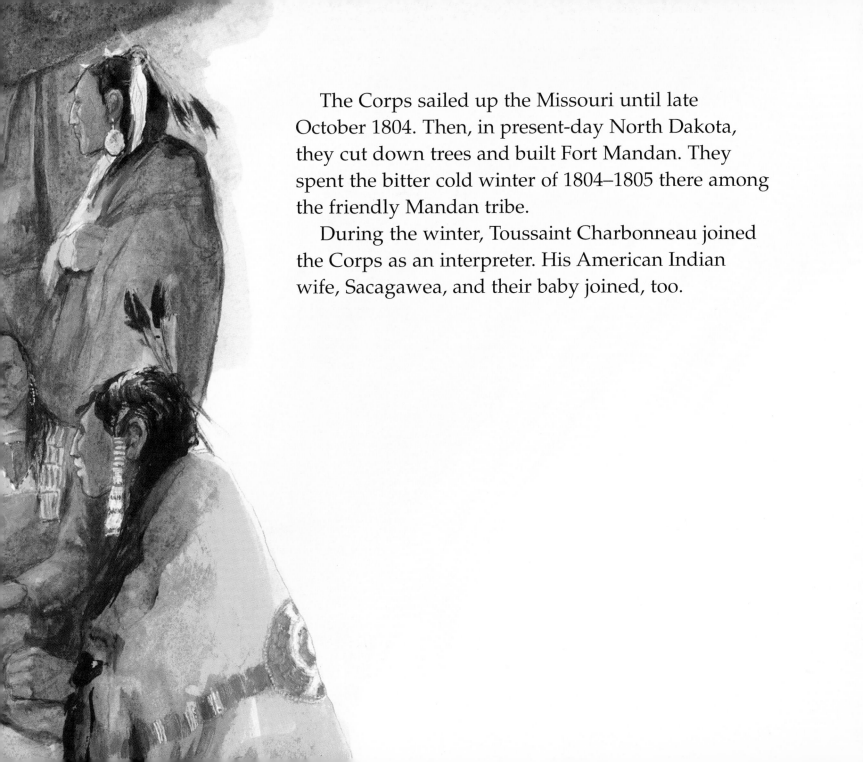

The Corps sailed up the Missouri until late October 1804. Then, in present-day North Dakota, they cut down trees and built Fort Mandan. They spent the bitter cold winter of 1804–1805 there among the friendly Mandan tribe.

During the winter, Toussaint Charbonneau joined the Corps as an interpreter. His American Indian wife, Sacagawea, and their baby joined, too.

Sacagawea became an important member of the expedition. When American Indians along the way saw her, "they pointed," Clark wrote. She "confirmed those people of our friendly intentions" for they knew "no woman ever accompanies a war party," especially not a woman with her baby.

By early spring, the frozen Missouri River began to melt. Lewis and Clark sent the large keelboat back to St. Louis with some of their men and with reports, along with boxes of animal skins, plants, stuffed birds, and snakes.

They set off again on April 7, 1805.
They met many American Indian tribes and
their chiefs. Lewis and Clark spoke with them, and
distributed gifts and peace tokens.

Lewis and Clark and their team saw the unspoiled beauty of the American frontier. Lewis wrote of "a most beautiful and extensive plain . . . [where] emense herds of buffalo are feeding."

Clark wrote of the many flowers they saw. "Nature appears to have exerted herself to beautify the scenery."

There were dangers, too. The men wrote of snake bites and troublesome mosquitoes and a large gnat, "which does not sting, but attacks the eye in swarms and compels us to brush them off or have our eyes filled with them."

In May 1805 six of the men encountered a grizzly bear. "This monster ran at them with open mouth," Lewis wrote. The men fired their rifles, but that didn't stop the grizzly. Two men threw their guns down and jumped into the river. The bear "plunged into the river only a few feet behind the second man." At last, Lewis wrote, "one of those who still remained on shore shot him [the bear] through the head and finally killed him."

The explorers suffered from the weather, too.
In the first winter Lewis recorded the temperature at forty-five degrees below zero. In November 1805 Clark wrote of a storm that "did not cease."

And there was triumph.

In August they reached the Continental Divide. On one side of the divide, the rivers flowed east, to the Atlantic Ocean. On the other side, they flowed west, to the Pacific.

"O! the joy," Clark wrote in November 1805. They were close to the west coast of the continent.

By mid November 1805 the Corps reached the Pacific Ocean. Shortly after that, members of the Corps voted on where to build their winter camp. Among those who voted were Clark's slave, York, and Sacagawea, long before blacks and women voted in the United States elections. They built their camp a few miles from the ocean near present-day Astoria, Oregon, and called it Fort Clatsop after the local tribe.

The Corps had crossed the American continent. With the coming of spring, it was time to go home. On March 23, 1806, they began their journey east.

In early July Lewis and three men separated from the others to explore a different route up the Marias River. While they camped, some of the Blackfoot tribe stole their rifles and there was a fight. Two of the tribe were killed. Peace between them and white men was shattered.

Later there was a shooting. One of the men was hunting meat and shot what he thought was an elk or a bear. But it was Lewis. He shot him in his rear and for weeks after that Lewis had difficulty walking.

In mid August Lewis and his men rejoined Clark and the rest of the Corps. On September 23, 1806, they reached St. Louis.

"It is with pleasure," Lewis wrote to Jefferson, "I announce to you the safe arrival of myself and party."

The president replied, "I received, my dear Sir, with unspeakable joy your letter of Sep. 23."

After thousands of miles of travel by water, horseback, and on foot, they had returned. They hadn't found woolly mammoths or a Northwest Passage, but they did come back with plant, rock, and animal specimens new to American scientists. They returned, too, with reports on many of the nation's American Indian neighbors.

In December President Jefferson wrote to Congress that the Corps of Discovery "had all the success which could have been expected. . . . Lewis and Clark, and their brave companions, have by this arduous service deserved well of their country."

Congress awarded the men of the expedition double pay.

After their return, Lewis and Clark separated. Lewis was made governor of the Louisiana Territory. Clark was made agent general for Indian Affairs for Louisiana and governor of the Missouri Territory.

Meriwether Lewis was upset by financial troubles and on October 11, 1809, was found dead of gunshot wounds. He was either killed by a robber or by his own hand.

William Clark married twice and had seven children. In 1838 he died in the St. Louis home of his eldest son, Meriwether Lewis Clark, named after his trusted colleague.

Meriwether Lewis and William Clark were American pioneers. They opened the west to the new nation.

AUTHOR'S NOTES

In 1783 Congressman Thomas Jefferson asked General George Rogers Clark, a Revolutionary War hero and William Clark's older brother, to lead an expedition west of the Mississippi River. George Rogers Clark wrote back, "It is what I think we ought to do," but he didn't want to do it.

In 1786, while he was minister to France, Jefferson suggested to John Ledyard that he travel across Europe and Asia, to Vancouver and the American coast. Ledyard started out, but in Siberia he was arrested as a spy.

In 1793, when he was secretary of state, Jefferson approached André Michaux, a Frenchman then settled in America. Michaux started out, but got only as far as Kentucky.

In 1802 President Jefferson sent agents to France to either purchase New Orleans or guarantee that American ships could travel freely through its port. Napoléon Bonaparte, the French ruler, offered instead to sell the entire Louisiana Territory including New Orleans, more than 800,000 square miles, for $15 million, just a few cents an acre.

On August 19, 1804, the Corps of Discovery had its one fatality. Sergeant Charles Floyd died of what Lewis called "biliose chorlick" but was probably appendicitis, incurable at the time.

At times, Sacagawea helped guide the Corps and interpret for the men. The name *Sacagawea* means "Bird Woman."

In 1806, when they returned to St. Louis, York asked to be freed. Clark refused, but years later he did grant York his freedom.

IMPORTANT DATES

1770 William Clark born in Caroline County, Virginia, August 1.

1774 Meriwether Lewis born in Albermarle County, Virginia, August 18.

1801 Lewis becomes the private secretary of President Jefferson.

1803 The United States buys the Louisiana Territory from France. Purchase announced July 4.

1804 The Corps of Discovery begins its journey, May 14.

Winter 1804–1805
The Corps sets up camp, Fort Mandan, at the mouth of the Knife River in present-day North Dakota.

1805 The Corps heads west again, April 7.

1805 The expedition reaches the Columbia River, October 16.

1805 The expedition reaches the Pacific Ocean in November.

1806 The expedition starts back, March 23.

1806 The expedition returns to St. Louis, September 23.

1809 Meriwether Lewis dies, October 11.

1838 William Clark dies, September 1.

FURTHER READING

Adler, David A. *A Picture Book of Sacagawea.* New York: Holiday House, 2000.

Kroll, Steven. *Lewis and Clark: Explorers of the American West.* New York: Holiday House, 1994.

Roop, Peter, and Connie Roop. *Off the Map: The Journals of Lewis and Clark.* New York: Walker, 1993.

Stein, Conrad. *Lewis and Clark.* Chicago: Children's Press, 1997.

SELECTED BIBLIOGRAPHY

Ambrose, Stephen E. *Undaunted Courage: Meriwether Lewis, Thomas Jefferson, and the Opening of the American West.* New York: Simon and Schuster, 1996.

Andrist, Ralph K. *To the Pacific with Lewis and Clark.* New York: American Heritage, 1967.

Blumberg, Rhoda. *The Incredible Journey of Lewis and Clark.* New York: Lothrop, 1987.

Cutright, Paul Russell. *A History of the Lewis and Clark Journals.* Norman: University of Oklahoma Press, 1976.

—. *Lewis and Clark: Pioneering Naturalists.* Urbana: University of Illinois Press, 1969.

DeVoto, Bernard, ed. *The Journals of Lewis and Clark.* Boston: Houghton Mifflin, 1953.

Duncan, Dayton, and Ken Burns. *Lewis and Clark: The Journal of the Corps of Discovery.* New York: Knopf, 1997.

Hawke, David Freeman. *Those Tremendous Mountains: The Story of the Lewis and Clark Expedition.* New York: Norton, 1980.

Holloway, David. *Lewis and Clark and the Crossing of North America.* New York: Saturday Review Press, 1974.

Jackson, Donald, ed. *Letters of the Lewis and Clark Expedition.* Urbana: University of Illinois Press, 1962.

Peterson, David, and Mark Coburn. *Meriwether Lewis and William Clark.* Chicago: Children's Press, 1988.

RECOMMENDED WEB SITES

www.pbs.org/lewisandclark
www.lewisandclark.net

www.lewisandclark.org
www.montanalewisandclark.org